CW01096114

AIR FRYER

Beginner

RECIPES

Thanks for purchasing your copy of the Air Frying Foodie Beginner Recipes Cookbook.

join the group

facebook.com/groups/easyairfryerrecipesgroup

weekly recipes

for weekly recipes, be sure to visit our page!
airfryingfoodie.com

We hope you enjoy these recipes!

Table of Contents

Breakfasts

A I R   F R Y E R
Breakfast Potatoes

PREP TIME: 10 minutes
COOK TIME: 20 minutes

INGREDIENTS:
- 4 Russet Potatoes
- 2 tbsp olive oil
- 1 tsp salt
- 1 tsp garlic powder
- 1 tsp paprika
- ½ tsp black pepper

1. Peel, rinse, and then cut the potatoes into 1 inch cubes, about the size of dice
2. Next, using a mixing bowl, toss the cubed potatoes in olive oil and then the seasonings, until they are well coated
3. Place the seasoned potatoes in the air fryer basket, and air fry at 400°F for 20 minutes, shaking the basket halfway through the cooking time
4. The potatoes should be golden brown and crispy when done
5. Serve while hot

AIR FRYER
Bacon

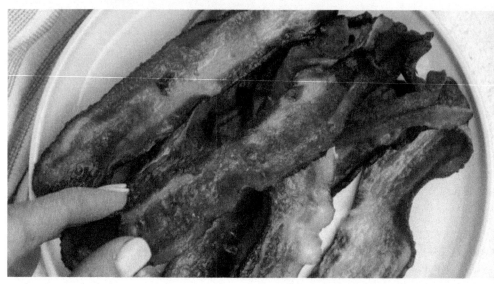

PREP TIME: 2 minutes
COOK TIME: 10 minutes

INGREDIENTS:
- 1 Package of Bacon

1. Preheat the Air Fryer to 400°F
2. Place the bacon slices in the basket of the air fryer in a single layer. (It's ok if the bacon slightly overlaps)
3. Close the basket door and cook at 400°F for 10 minutes
4. Check the bacon after 10 minutes for crispiness. If you would like the bacon to be crispier, add another minute or two of cook time
5. Remove to a plate and blot with paper towels to soak up any excess grease before serving

AIR FRYER
French Toast

PREP TIME: 5 minutes
COOK TIME: 10-12 minutes

INGREDIENTS:
- 4 pieces bread
- 2 large eggs
- 1 ½ tbsp milk
- 2 tbsp sugar
- ½ tsp cinnamon

1. In a small bowl, combine the sugar and cinnamon. Set aside
2. In a medium bowl, add eggs and milk and whisk together. Pour the egg mixture in a rimmed shallow bowl for easier dipping
3. Take a slice of bread and dip it into the egg mixture, coating both sides
4. Add a sprinkle of cinnamon and sugar to each piece of bread, and then place the bread slices, in the prepared air fryer basket. Do not stack slices
5. Air fry the French toast for 8-10 minutes at 390°F, carefully flipping the toast after 5 minutes
6. Once golden brown and fully cooked, remove the toast from the air fryer.

7

A I R   F R Y E R
French Toast Sticks

PREP TIME: 4 minutes
COOK TIME: 8 minutes

INGREDIENTS:
- 4-6 pieces bread*
- 2 eggs
- 3 tbsp granulated
- sugar
- 2 tsp cinnamon

*Allow bread to sit out for 2-3 hours before using

1. Mix the cinnamon and sugar together in a small bowl or plate and set aside
2. Stack the bread and then use a serrated knife to cut the slices into thirds
3. Whisk the eggs together and pour them into a rimmed plate
4. Dip the bread pieces into the egg and then dip into the cinnamon and sugar
5. Place the bread into the prepared Air Fryer basket in a single layer
6. Air Fryer the bread pieces for 8-9 minutes on 370°F, flipping them halfway
7. Remove from the Air Fryer and serve immediately

A I R F R Y E R
Egg Bites

PREP TIME: 5 minutes
COOK TIME: 10 minutes

INGREDIENTS:
- 6 large eggs
- 1 tbsp milk
- 4 slices bacon crumbled
- 1/2 cup cheddar cheese
- 1/2 tsp salt
- 1/4 tsp pepper
- 1 green onion chopped

1. In a large bowl, combine the eggs and milk, and whisk together
2. Add in the crumbled bacon, grated cheddar cheese, onions, and seasonings, stirring to combine
3. Equally divide the egg mixture into silicone cups, about 2/3 full, leaving room for them to rise
4. Place in the air fryer, air fry at 300°F for 8-10 minutes

AIR FRYER
Monkey Bread

PREP TIME: 3 minutes
COOK TIME: 20 minutes

INGREDIENTS:
- 1 can biscuit dough
- 1/4 cup granulated sugar
- 1/4 cup brown sugar
- 1 1/2 cups powdered sugar
- 5 tbsp heavy cream
- 1/2 tsp vanilla extract

1. Preheat Air Fryer to 320°F
2. Cut dough into small pieces, and place in large plastic Ziploc bag. Add the sugar and brown sugar to the bag, and toss the bag to coat pieces
3. Place coated biscuit dough pieces into Bundt pan. Air Fryer at 320°F for 18-20 minutes
4. To prepare the glaze, stir the powdered sugar, heavy cream, and vanilla flavoring together
5. Remove pan from the air fryer once it's finished cooking. Allow bread to cool for 5 minutes. Then, flip the monkey bread out of the Bundt pan onto a serving plate and top it with the homemade glaze

AIR FRYER
Eggs in a Basket

PREP TIME: 1 minutes
COOK TIME: 9 minutes

INGREDIENTS:
- 2 slice bread
- 2 eggs

1. Preheat the Air Fryer to 330°F
2. Once preheated, spray the basket with non-stick cooking spray, or line with parchment paper
3. Using a large cookie cutter, cut a hole in the center of each slice of bread. Place the bread in air fryer basket
4. Crack the egg and add it to the center of the slice of bread
5. Air fry for 5 minutes on 330°F. Use a spatula and carefully flip the egg in a hole and cook for an additional 3-4 minutes
6. Remove from the Air Fryer and top with a pinch of salt and pepper before serving

AIR FRYER
Breakfast Bowl

PREP TIME: 5 MINUTES
COOK TIME: 16 MINUTES

INGREDIENTS:
- 5 chicken nuggets frozen
- 10 tater tots frozen
- 4 eggs scrambled
- 1/4 cup milk
- 1/4 cup shredded cheddar cheese
- salt and pepper to taste

1. Preheat the Air Fryer to 400°F
2. Add the chicken nuggets and tater tots to the Air Fryer and cook at 400°F for 6 minutes
3. While the chicken and tots are cooking, whisk the eggs and milk in small bowl, until fully combined
4. Once the chicken and tots are finished cooking, chop them into small bite-sized pieces
5. Pour the egg mixture into a 7" springform pan. Top the egg mixture with the chicken and tots
6. Decrease heat to 350°F and place the pan in the air fryer basket Cook for 7 minutes. Stir, then cook for an additional 3 minutes
7. Top with shredded cheese and heat for an additional minute

A I R   F R Y E R
Banana Muffins

PREP TIME: 5 minutes
COOK TIME: 8 minutes

INGREDIENTS:
- 1 1/2 cups all purpose flour
- 1/2 cup granulated sugar
- 1/3 cup light brown sugar
- 1 tsp baking powder
- 2 ripe bananas, mashed
- 1/2 tsp vanilla extract
- 1 egg
- 1/3 cup butter, melted

1. In a large bowl, combine the flour and baking powder, then set aside
2. In a medium sized mixing bowl, cream together the white sugar, brown sugar, and butter with a hand mixer
3. Add the egg and the vanilla extract to the butter mixture
4. Pour the butter and sugar mixture into the flour mixture and mix until combined
5. Fold the mashed bananas into the muffin batter
6. Use a large cookie scoop or ice cream scoop to scoop the batter into the silicone baking molds. Fill each mold ¾ of the way full
7. Place the silicone molds into the basket of the air fryer and bake at 350°F for 6-8 minutes

AIR FRYER
Blueberry Muffin Bites

PREP TIME: 5 minutes
COOK TIME: 6 minutes

INGREDIENTS:
- 1 cup all purpose flour
- 3 tbsp sugar
- ½ tsp cinnamon
- ⅓ cup milk
- ¼ cup unsalted butter, melted (half a stick)
- 1 large egg
- 1 tsp vanilla
- ½ cup fresh or frozen blueberries

1. In a large bowl, combine the flour, sugar, and cinnamon in a bowl
2. Pour in the milk, melted butter, egg, and vanilla. Stir together with a fork until all of the ingredients are well combined
3. Gently fold in the blueberries to the batter, until they are evenly distributed
4. Using a portion scoop, fill the silicone cups about ¾ of the way. If using a small muffin tin, fill paper liners ¾ of the way
5. Gently place into the basket. Air fry at 350°F for 4-6 minutes

Entrées

A I R   F R Y E R
Chicken Breast

PREP TIME: 5 minutes
COOK TIME: 20 minutes

INGREDIENTS:
- 4 boneless chicken breasts
- 1 tbsp olive oil
- 1/2 tsp kosher salt
- 1/2 tsp thyme
- 1/2 tsp rosemary
- 1/2 tsp sage
- 1/4 tsp black pepper

Optional: 1 tsp parsley

1. Use a paper towel to pat the chicken dry
2. In a small or shallow bowl, combine the spice mixture with the olive oil and then brush the chicken with oil mixture on both sides
3. Once each piece of chicken is coated with olive oil and seasonings, place the pieces of chicken in a single layer in the air fryer basket
4. Next, you cook at 380°F for 8-10 minutes on each side
5. Cook until golden brown, and the chicken has an internal temperature of 165°F

AIR FRYER
Turkey Meatballs

PREP TIME: 5 minutes
COOK TIME: 10 minutes

INGREDIENTS:
- 1 1/2 lbs ground turkey
- 1 medium bell pepper red
- 1/2 cup Italian parsley chopped
- 1 large egg
- 1 tbsp Italian seasoning
- 1/2 tsp salt
- 1/2 tsp ground black pepper

1. Preheat the Air Fryer to 400°F
2. Add ground turkey, bell pepper, parsley, egg, and seasonings to a bowl. Mix well
3. Use a scoop or a tablespoon to shape each meatball into 1 1/4" balls
4. Place the meatballs in a single layer in the prepared air fryer basket
5. Cook at 400°F for 8-10 minutes, or until cooked through
6. Remove the cooked meatballs from the air fryer and continue to cook the remaining meatballs

AIR FRYER
Brats and Peppers

PREP TIME: 4 minutes
COOK TIME: 11 minutes

INGREDIENTS:
- 1 package Bratwurst sausage
- 3 bell peppers

1. Remove the brats from the refrigerator and allow them to sit at room temperature for 10-15 minutes
2. Slice the bell peppers, (optional: mix with oil and seasonings) and set aside
3. Prepare the basket of the air fryer with a nonstick spray such as olive oil or use parchment paper for easier clean up
4. Place the brats in the prepared air fryer basket in a single layer. Place the sliced bell peppers around the sides
5. Cook on 360°F for 10-12 minutes, flipping the bell peppers halfway through, until the brats have reached an internal temperature of 160° F

A I R   F R Y E R
Country Style Ribs

PREP TIME: 5 minutes
COOK TIME: 20 minutes

INGREDIENTS:
- 2 lbs ribs country-style
- 1 tsp smoked paprika
- 1 1/2 tsp garlic powder
- 2 tsp ground black pepper
- 5 ounces barbecue sauce

1. Pat ribs dry and rub with seasonings
2. Preheat the air fryer to 380°F
3. Prepare the basket of the air fryer with nonstick cooking spray
4. Place the ribs in a single layer in the basket of the air fryer Cook at 380°F 20 minutes
5. Remove the basket and brush barbecue sauce onto the tops and sides of the ribs Return to air fryer and cook for an additional 2 minutes
6. Check the internal temperature with a meat thermometer to ensure the pork has reached 145°F

19

A I R   F R Y E R
Grilled Ham and Cheese

PREP TIME: 5 minutes
COOK TIME: 12 minutes

INGREDIENTS:
- 8 slices bread
- 4 slices ham
- 4 slices cheese
- 1 tablespoon butter softened

For traditional grilled cheese sandwich, omit ham

1. Spread a light layer of butter on one side of each piece of bread
2. Assemble the sandwiches by adding one slice of cheese and one slice of ham, or preferred deli meats in between two pieces of bread, butter sides out
3. Place prepared sandwiches into air fryer basket, without stacking
4. Air fry at 370°F for 10-12 minutes, until the bread is golden and reaches your desired crispness, flipping sandwiches halfway through cooking

A I R   F R Y E R
Whole Chicken

PREP TIME: 5 minutes
COOK TIME: 60 minutes

INGREDIENTS:
- 4-5lb Whole Chicken
- 1 tbsp Italian seasoning
- ½ tsp Paprika
- ½ tsp Ground Black Pepper

1. Preheat the Air Fryer to 360°F. Once preheated, prepare the liner of the basket with non stick cooking spray
2. Clean the chicken and remove any innards that are in the cavity of the chicken. Rub the seasonings all over the chicken, covering it well
3. Place the seasoned chicken into the prepared Air Fryer basket, breast side down, and cook for 25 minutes. Flip the chicken to cook breast side up, and cook for an additional 40 minutes
4. Insert a thermometer into the thickest part of the chicken breast. Temperature should reach 165°F or higher

AIR FRYER
Garlic Steak Bites

PREP TIME: 5 minutes
COOK TIME: 10 minutes

INGREDIENTS:
- 3 lbs steak
- 2 tbsp garlic powder
- 1 tsp ground black pepper
- 1 tsp avocado oil

Adjust cooking times according to preference:

7- 8 minutes for medium-rare
10 minutes for a medium-medium well
10-12 minutes for well done

1. Preheat the Air Fryer to 400°F
2. Cut up the steak into bite sized pieces
3. Season the steak bites with garlic powder and ground black pepper
4. Place the seasoned steak bites in a single layer in the air fryer basket
5. Cook for ten minutes, flipping and tossing the steak bites halfway through
6. Remove the steak bites from the air fryer basket and serve as desired

A I R   F R Y E R
Garlic Butter Shrimp

PREP TIME: 5 minutes
COOK TIME: 8 minutes

INGREDIENTS:
- 1 pound raw shrimp peeled and de-veined
- ¼ cup unsalted butter
- 2 cloves garlic minced, about 1 teaspoon

1. If not already prepared, remove shells, rinse the shrimp and pat them dry. Place them in a large bowl, and set aside
2. In a small microwave safe bowl, combine the butter and minced garlic, and microwave for about 30 seconds, until the butter has melted
3. Pour the butter and garlic mixture over the shrimp, and stir together, coating the shrimp with the mixture
4. Pour the shrimp into the basket, leaving enough room between them so they aren't stacked
5. Air fry at 370°F for 6-8 minutes, tossing halfway through

A I R   F R Y E R
BBQ Chicken Wings

PREP TIME: 5 minutes
COOK TIME: 20 minutes

INGREDIENTS:
- 24 chicken wings
- 1 Tbsp garlic powder
- 2 Tbsp brown sugar
- ⅔ cup BBQ sauce

HINT:

For extra crispy wings, add a pinch of baking powder to the seasoning before coating the wings

1. Preheat the Air Fryer to 380°F
2. Rinse and completely dry the chicken wings
3. Mix the garlic powder and brown sugar together and use as a dry rub over the wings
4. Place the wings in a single layer in the basket of the air fryer
5. Cook the wings at 380°F for 16 minutes, flipping the wings every 4 minutes
6. Increase the heat to 400°F and cook for an additional 4 minutes. Use a meat thermometer to ensure the wings have reached 165°F. Add 1-2 minutes time if needed
7. Remove wings and toss with BBQ sauce until they are completely coated in sauce

AIR FRYER
Chicken Fajitas

PREP TIME: 5 minutes
COOK TIME: 18 minutes

INGREDIENTS:
- 3 boneless skinless chicken breasts
- 1 red bell pepper
- 1 orange bell pepper
- 1 yellow bell peppers
- 1 onion
- 4 tbsp taco seasoning

1. Preheat the Air Fryer to 380°F
2. Prepare the basket with nonstick spray once the Air Fryer has completed the preheat cycle
3. Slice the chicken and all vegetables into slices. Add the slices to a medium sized mixing bowl and top with taco seasoning
4. Add the seasoning chicken and vegetables to the prepared Air Fryer basket and cook at 380°F for 18 minutes
5. Toss the chicken and vegetables every few minutes to ensure even cooking
6. Remove the chicken and vegetables from the Air Fryer and serve with flour tortillas, cheese, and your favorite fajita toppings

AIR FRYER
Pork Chops

PREP TIME: 5 minutes
COOK TIME: 12 minutes

INGREDIENTS:
- 3 pork chops thick cut
- ½ tsp black pepper
- ¼ tsp paprika
- ¼ tsp garlic powder
- ¼ tsp onion powder

1. Preheat the Air Fryer to 400°F
2. Combine the seasonings to a small bowl and then use your hands to rub the seasoning over the pork chops, fully covering the front, back, and sides of each chop
3. Prepare the Air Fryer basket with non stick spray or parchment paper, and then line the pork chops in the bottom of the air fryer basket in a single layer. Leave room for air circulation between each pork chop
4. Cook at 400°F for 6 minutes. Flip the pork chops and continue to cook for an additional 8-10 minutes. Add 1-2 minutes cooking time until internal temperature has reached 145°F

A I R   F R Y E R
Taco Casserole

PREP TIME: 10 minutes
COOK TIME: 20 minutes

INGREDIENTS:
- 1 lb lean ground beef 95% lean
- 3 tbsp taco seasoning
- ¼ cup water
- ½ cup bell pepper chopped
- 10 ounces diced tomatoes and green chilis not drained
- 4 large eggs
- ¼ cup sour cream
- ⅓ cup heavy cream
- ½ cup cheddar cheese shredded

Optional: 1 tbsp green onions

1. In medium skillet, brown the ground beef
2. Add bell pepper, diced tomatoes with green chilis, water, and taco seasoning to ground beef. Simmer for additional 3 minutes.
3. Preheat air fryer at 300° F
4. In medium mixing bowl, whisk together the eggs, sour cream, and heavy cream, set aside.
5. Pour meat mixture into casserole dish. Add the egg mixture to the top of the meat mixture.
6. Add the casserole dish to the preheated air fryer basket and cook at 300° F for 18 minutes.
7. Add shredded cheddar cheese and cook for an additional 2 minutes or until the cheese is melted. **27**

AIR FRYER
Hamburgers

PREP TIME: 4 minutes
COOK TIME: 12 minutes

INGREDIENTS:
- 4 hamburger patties

1. Preheat the Air Fryer to 370°F
2. Prepare the Air Fryer basket with nonstick cooking spray
3. Add the hamburger patties into the Air Fryer basket in a single layer
4. Cook in the preheated fryer for 6 minutes Flip the hamburger patties and cook for an additional 5-7 minutes, depending on how well done you would like the hamburgers
5. Carefully remove the hamburger patties from the Air Fryer basket and serve with your favorite sides and toppings

AIR FRYER
Honey Mustard Salmon

PREP TIME: 5 minutes
COOK TIME: 12 minutes

INGREDIENTS:
- 2-4 portions Salmon 4-6 ounces each
- 1 tbsp olive oil
- ½ tsp salt
- ½ tsp pepper
- 2 tbsp Dijon Mustard
- 2 tbsp Honey

1. Lightly brush or spray the bottom of the basket with olive oil
2. Place salmon portions in the basket and season with salt and pepper to your preference
3. In a small bowl, stir the honey and Dijon mustard together
4. Use a brush or a spoon, and evenly coat the tops of each salmon portion with the honey mustard mixture
5. Close the basket and cook at 380°F for 10-12 minutes
6. Check for doneness using a fork. Salmon should flake when fully cooked

29

A I R   F R Y E R
Ribeye Steak

PREP TIME: 5 minutes
COOK TIME: 16 minutes

INGREDIENTS:
- 2 rib eye steaks 16 ounces each
- 1 tbsp olive oil
- ½ tsp pepper
- ½ tsp salt

Blue Cheese Butter
- 2 tbsp unsalted butter melted
- 1 tbsp blue cheese crumbled

1. To prepare butter topping, melt butter and blue cheese in the microwave, for about 30 seconds. Stir together, and return to refrigerator while steak is cooking
2. Lightly coat steak with olive oil, on both sides and then add salt and pepper, or your preferred seasonings
3. Preheat air fryer to 400°F
4. Cook at 400°F, for 6-8 minutes on each side, depending on preference for doneness
5. Let steak sit for 5-10 minutes before serving and top with spoonful of prepared butter

A I R   F R Y E R
Chicken Thighs

PREP TIME: 5 minutes
COOK TIME: 20 minutes

INGREDIENTS:
- 4-5 chicken thighs bone in, skin on
- 1 tbsp olive oil
- 1 tsp ground black pepper
- 1 tsp onion powder
- 1 tsp garlic powder
- ½ tsp cinnamon

1. Preheat the air fryer to 400°F
2. Rinse and pat the chicken thighs dry with a paper towel. Place the chicken in a small bowl and toss in the olive oil
3. Add the seasonings to the chicken thighs and make sure to cover them evenly
4. Place the thighs into the air fryer basket in a single layer
5. Air Fry at 400°F for 15 minutes of cooking time. Flip the chicken thighs and cook for an additional 8 minutes
6. Use a meat thermometer to ensure the thighs have reached an internal temperature of 165°F
7. For a crispier skin, cook for an additional 1-2 minutes before serving

AIR FRYER
Turkey Breast

PREP TIME: 5 minutes
COOK TIME: 60 minutes

INGREDIENTS:
- 3–4 lbs boneless turkey breast
- 2 tbsp unsalted butter melted
- ½ tsp salt
- ½ tsp thyme
- ½ tsp rosemary
- ½ tsp sage
- ¼ tsp black pepper

1. Use a paper towel to pat the turkey dry
2. In a small bowl, combine the seasonings with the melted butter. Brush the butter and completely coat the turkey on both sides
3. Place the turkey in the air fryer basket, or on a baking tray and place in the air fryer
4. Air fry at 350°F for 30 minutes on each side. Confirm doneness with a meat thermometer. Internal temperature should reach 165°F.
5. Let turkey rest for about 5 minutes before carving

A I R   F R Y E R
Teriyaki Pork Chops

PREP TIME: 5 minutes
COOK TIME: 16 minutes

INGREDIENTS:
- 4 pork loin chops ½ –¾ inch thick
- 2 tbsp horseradish sauce
- ⅓ cup Teriyaki marinade and sauce
- 1/4 tsp cinnamon
- 1 tsp sesame seeds

1. Combine the teriyaki sauce, horseradish sauce, and cinnamon
2. Pour the sauce into a Ziploc bag and add the pork chops. Seal the bag, and then shake the pork chops so they are coated with the sauce
3. Place the bag in the refrigerator, and allow the pork chops to marinate in the sauce for at least 30 minutes to an hour
4. After they have marinated, remove them from the bag, and place them in the air fryer. Brush again with sauce when flipping chops halfway through cooking. Then discard any remaining sauce
5. Air fry at 400°F for 6-8 minutes on each side. Pork chops should reach internal temperature of 145°F

A I R   F R Y E R
Buffalo Wings

PREP TIME: 5 minutes
COOK TIME: 22 minutes

INGREDIENTS:
- 24 wings
- 1 cup olive oil
- 1 tbsp ground black pepper
- 2 tsp onion powder
- 2 tsp garlic powder

Buffalo Wing Sauce
- 1 cup Louisiana Hot Sauce
- ½ cup margarine
- 4 tbsp water
- 2 tsp paprika
- 4 tsp granulated sugar
- ¼ tsp garlic powder
- ¼ tsp onion powder

1. Preheat Air Fryer to 360°F
2. Add wings, olive oil, and seasonings to a large sealable plastic bag. Seal and toss the wings to coat evenly
3. Air Fry at 360°F for 18 minutes, flipping the wings every 5-6 minutes
4. Increase temperature to 390°F and cook for additional 2 minutes. Wings should have internal temperature of 165°F
5. Add sauce ingredients to a sauce pan and bring to a boil. Quickly remove from heat and cover. Let rest for 5 minutes
6. Add the fully cooked wings to a medium sized mixing bowl and toss with the sauce

A I R F R Y E R
Filet Mignon

PREP TIME: 5 minutes
COOK TIME: 12 minutes

INGREDIENTS:
- 2 filet mignon 4-6 ounces each
- 1 tbsp olive oil
- ½ tsp pepper
- ½ tsp salt

Blue Cheese Butter
- 2 tbsp unsalted butter melted
- 1 tbsp blue cheese crumbled

1. To prepare butter topping, melt butter and blue cheese in the microwave, for about 30 seconds. Stir together, and return to refrigerator while steak is cooking

2. Pat steaks dry, then coat the steaks with oil on the top and bottom of each piece

3. Season with salt and pepper, according to your preferences

4. Transfer steaks to the air fryer basket. Air fry at at 380°F for 10 to 12 minutes. Flip steaks halfway through cooking

5. Use meat thermometer to confirm preferred doneness. Once cooked, for extra tender steak, let steak rest for about 5-10 minutes before eating

35

Appetizers

AIR FRYER
Jalapeño Poppers

PREP TIME: 10 minutes
COOK TIME: 12 minutes

INGREDIENTS:
- 6 medium Jalapeños
- 4 ounces cream cheese, softened
- 6–12 slices bacon

1. Cut the jalapeños in half, lengthwise. Remove all of the seeds and rinse the jalapeños
2. Cut small slices of the cream cheese, in strips, and place a strip inside each half piece of the pepper
3. Wrap a piece of bacon around the stuffed pepper and secure with a toothpick
4. Place the stuffed peppers, without stacking or overlapping, in the basket of the air fryer. Work in batches if necessary
5. Cook at 370°F for 10-12 minutes, until the bacon is cooked to your desired crispness

A I R   F R Y E R
Coconut Shrimp

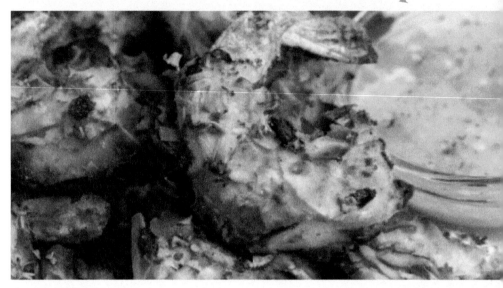

PREP TIME: 10 minutes
COOK TIME: 10 minutes

INGREDIENTS:
- 25 large shrimp peeled and deveined
- 1/2 cup coconut flour
- 1 3/4 cup coconut flakes unsweetened
- 3 eggs
- 1 tbsp ground black pepper
- 1 tsp smoked paprika
- 1 tsp salt

1. Preheat Air Fryer to 390°F
2. Lightly spray air fryer basket with non stick cooking spray
3. Arrange three bowls. Add coconut flour, paprika, salt and pepper to first bowl. Coconut flakes to the second bowl, and then whisk eggs and add to third bowl
4. Dip shrimp into coconut flour mixture, then egg mixture, and finally into coconut flakes. Set aside on a wire rack until all shrimp are coated
5. Add shrimp in single layer to air fryer basket. Air fry at 380°F for 8-10 minutes. Flip the shrimp halfway through cooking
6. Remove when golden brown

A I R   F R Y E R
Ham and Cheese Sliders

PREP TIME: 5 minutes
COOK TIME: 8 minutes

INGREDIENTS:
- 1 package Hawaiian Sweet Rolls one dozen
- 1/4 cup mayonnaise
- 1/4 cup honey mustard
- 12 slices ham
- 6 slices swiss cheese
- 3 tbsp butter melted
- 2 tbsp brown sugar
- 2 tsp Worcestershire Sauce
- 1 tsp onion powder
- 1/2 tsp garlic powder

1. Cut the Hawaiian Rolls in half. Spread mustard on one side of the roll, and mayonnaise on the other side
2. Fold slices of cheese then cut in half. Add cheese and ham slices between rolls
3. Combine the melted butter with the brown sugar, Westchester sauce, onion powder, garlic powder, and poppy seeds. Stir the ingredients together
4. Place the rolls, in a single layer, in the air fryer basket, without stacking. Brush the sauce over the rolls.
5. Air fry at 300°F for 5 to 8 minutes until the cheese has melted, and the sandwiches are golden brown

39

AIR FRYER
Crab Cakes

PREP TIME: 5 minutes
COOK TIME: 10 minutes

INGREDIENTS:
- 12 oz crab
- 2 eggs
- 3 tbsp mayo
- ½ bell pepper red
- ½ cup breadcrumbs
- ¼ tsp garlic salt
- ¼ tsp black pepper

1. Preheat the air fryer to 390°F
2. Add crab, eggs, breadcrumbs, diced bell pepper, mayo, and seasonings to a medium sized mixing bowl. Mix until combined
3. Measure out patties with ½ cup measuring cup and keep them no thicker than 1" thickness
4. Add the crab patties to the prepared air fryer basket. Spray the tops of the patties. Cook at 390°F for 8 minutes
5. Spray the top of the patties and cook for an additional 1-2 minutes. The tops should be a crispy golden brown
6. Garnish with fresh green onion tops and serve with tarter sauce

A I R   F R Y E R
Salmon Cakes

PREP TIME: 10 minutes
COOK TIME: 10 minutes

INGREDIENTS:
- 14.75 oz salmon canned, deboned
- 2 eggs
- 1 tbsp mayonnaise
- 1/2 bell pepper red
- 1/2 cup breadcrumbs
- 1/2 tsp garlic powder
- 1/2 tsp black pepper
- 1/4 tsp salt
- 2 tbsp fresh chopped parsley
- 1 tsp olive oil spray

1. Preheat the air fryer to 390°F
2. Mix the salmon, breadcrumbs, eggs, and seasonings in a large bowl.
3. Measure out the salmon patties with ½ cup measuring cup.
4. Form the salmon cakes to be no larger than 1" thickness.
5. Add the salmon cakes to the prepared air fryer basket. Spray the tops of the patties and cook for 8 minutes.
6. Open the Air Fryer and flip the patties over, spray the top of the patties, and cook for an additional 2 minutes.
7. Serve with dill sauce or favorite dipping sauce.

A I R   F R Y E R
BBQ Little Smokies

PREP TIME: 5 minutes
COOK TIME: 10 minutes

INGREDIENTS:

- 12 oz Little Smokies
- ¼ cup BBQ sauce
- 2 tbsp brown sugar

1. Add the Smokies to the prepared air fryer basket and cook at 350°F for 6 minutes. Toss halfway through
2. Brush the smokies with BBQ sauce and then sprinkle the brown sugar over the top. Cook for an additional 2-3 minutes.
3. Carefully remove the sausages from the air fryer and serve

A I R   F R Y E R
Pesto Pinwheels

PREP TIME: 5 minutes
COOK TIME: 13 minutes

INGREDIENTS:
- 1 Puff Pastry Sheet
- 2 tbsp Basil Pesto
- 4 ounces Black Forest Ham About 8 Slices
- ¼ cup Parmesan Cheese Shredded

1. Thaw one puff pastry sheet. Roll to a rectangle shape
2. Spoon pesto sauce onto the pastry sheet, covering as much as possible. Layer ham slices, covering pest sauce, then top with parmesan cheese
3. Starting with long end, tightly roll the pastry. Cut the roll into 12 pieces and place in lined, or lightly sprayed air fryer basket, with the cut side down. Do not stack or overlap pinwheels.
4. Cook at 350°F with a cooking time of 13-15 minutes, until they are golden brown

Potato Skins

PREP TIME: 5 minutes
COOK TIME: 45 minutes

INGREDIENTS:
- 4 medium baked potatoes
- ½ cup shredded cheddar cheese
- 4 strips cooked bacon crumbled
- ½ cup sour cream

1. Slice each baked potato in half. Scoop out most of the inside of the potato, leaving about ¼ inch of potato
2. Sprinkle each half with cheddar cheese and bacon crumbles
3. Place the potatoes in the air fryer basket, and air fry at 350°F for about 3-5 minutes, until the cheese melts
4. Serve with your favorite toppings

BBQ Chicken Pizza Rolls

PREP TIME: 5 minutes
COOK TIME: 6 minutes

INGREDIENTS:

- 1 can Crescent Dough Sheet 8 ounces
- ½ cup BBQ Sauce
- ½ tsp garlic powder
- ½ tsp red pepper flakes
- 1 can precooked chicken 12.5 ounces
- 1 ½ cup mozzarella cheese
- 4 slices cooked bacon crumbled
- 2 green onions chopped

1. Roll out pastry sheet to a rectangle, brushing BBQ sauce on top of the sheet
2. Sprinkle red pepper flakes and garlic powder, and mozzarella cheese over the sauce
3. Drain the can of chicken and spread the chicken over the cheese
4. Top the pizza with chopped onion and crumbled bacon, then, tightly roll the the dough lengthwise
5. Slice the roll into eight pieces and place in lightly sprayed air fryer basket, cut side down
6. Air fry at 370°F for about 5-6 minutes, until the crust is golden

AIR FRYER
Soft Pretzels

PREP TIME: 10 minutes
COOK TIME: 14 minutes

INGREDIENTS:
- 2 ¼ cups all purpose flour
- 1 tsp sugar
- 2 tsps salt
- 1 tbsp dry yeast
- 1 cup warm water
- 2 tbsp unsalted butter melted

Egg Wash
- 1 large egg
- 1 tsp water

1. In a large bowl, combine flour, sugar, salt, and yeast
2. Pour in the warm water and melted butter. Stir together with a fork until the dough begins to thicken and looks flaky
3. Remove the dough from the bowl. On a lightly floured surface, knead the dough until it becomes smooth. Form the dough into a ball shape
4. Cut the ball of dough into 8 pieces and then roll into ropes
5. Twist each rope into a pretzel shape and place into lightly sprayed air fryer basket
6. Combine egg and water, then brush on top of pretzels
7. Air fry at 320°F for 12-14 minutes, until golden brown

AIR FRYER
Spiced Pecans

PREP TIME: 10 minutes
COOK TIME: 5 minutes

INGREDIENTS:
- 2 cups pecans
- 1 tablespoon soy sauce
- 1 tablespoon brown sugar
- ¼ teaspoon salt
- ⅛ teaspoon cayenne pepper

1. In a medium bowl, combine the pecans with the soy sauce, brown sugar, and seasonings. Stir together to coat the pecans
2. Let the pecans sit for about 5-10 minutes
3. Light coat the air fryer basket with olive oil, or parchment paper liner
4. Cook at 325°F for about 3 to 5 minutes, shaking the basket halfway
5. Allow the pecans to cool

Side Dishes

AIR FRYER
Cornbread

PREP TIME: 5 minutes
COOK TIME: 15 minutes

INGREDIENTS:
- 1 ¼ cup all purpose flour
- ¾ cup cornmeal
- 3 tbsp sugar
- 1 tsp baking powder
- ¼ tsp salt
- 1 cup buttermilk
- ¼ cup unsalted butter melted
- 1 large egg

1. Using a medium bowl, combine the flour, cornmeal, flour, sugar, baking powder, and salt. Stir the dry ingredients together
2. Add in the buttermilk, melted butter, and egg. Continue to stir the ingredients together into a thick batter
3. Fill a 6x6 baking dish, or silicone cups ¾ full, with the cornbread batter.
4. Place in the air fryer basket
5. Air fryer at 350°F for 13-15 minutes, until they are golden brown

A I R   F R Y E R
Green Beans

PREP TIME: 5 minutes
COOK TIME: 10 minutes

INGREDIENTS:
- 1 pound Green Beans
- 1 tbsp olive oil
- 1 tsp salt
- ½ tsp black pepper

1. Trim the ends of the green beans, then rinse in water
2. In a large bowl combine the beans with olive oil, salt and optional black pepper. Toss the ingredients together until they beans are coated
3. Transfer them to the air fryer basket, and then lay them in a single layer. Work in batches if necessary. (One pound green beans is usually two batches.)
4. Air Fry at 400°F for 8-10 minutes, tossing one or two times during cooking, until they reach the desired crispness you prefer
5. Remove the beans with tongs, and add additional salt, parmesan cheese, or your favorite extra seasonings

A I R   F R Y E R
Hasselback Potatoes

PREP TIME: 10 minutes
COOK TIME: 40 minutes

INGREDIENTS:
- 4 medium Russet potatoes
- 4 tbsp olive oil extra virgin
- 1 tsp ground black pepper
- ½ tsp kosher salt
- 1 tsp garlic powder
- 1 tsp onion powder
- 2 tbsp parmesan cheese optional
- 1 tbsp parsley chopped, fresh, optional

1. Preheat Air Fryer to 350°F. Prepare the Air Fryer basket with nonstick cooking spray, olive oil spray, or parchment paper
2. Slice the potatoes into ¼" sections, careful not to cut all the way through the potato
3. Add olive oil and seasoning to a small bowl and mix well until combined
4. Use a pastry brush and brush half of the mixture onto the potatoes
5. Bake the potatoes at 350°F for 20 minutes. Open the basket and brush the remainder of the mixture to the potatoes and continue to cook for an additional 20 minutes
6. Remove from the Air Fryer and sprinkle parmesan cheese and fresh parsley before serving

AIR FRYER
Mexican Street Corn

PREP TIME: 5 minutes
COOK TIME: 10 minutes

INGREDIENTS:
- 4 corn on the cob
- 1 tsp chili powder
- 2 tbsp cilantro fresh, chopped
- ½ tsp salt
- ½ tsp ground black pepper
- ½ cup Feta cheese
- 1 tsp lime juice freshly squeezed, optional

1. Add the corn to air fryer basket.
2. Brush both sides of the corn with the melted butter
3. Air Fry the corn at 400°F for 10 minutes, flipping the corn halfway through the cook time
4. Add the chili powder, salt, and pepper to the remaining butter. Mix until combined
5. Brush the seasoned butter onto the cooked corn. Top the corn with the crumbled Feta cheese and then garnish with fresh cilantro and lime juice before serving

A I R   F R Y E R
Sweet Potato Casserole

PREP TIME: 5 minutes
COOK TIME: 10 minutes

INGREDIENTS:
- 29 ounce sweet potato yams drained
- ¾ cup pecans
- ¼ tsp salt
- 1 egg
- ½ tsp vanilla extract
- ¼ tsp ground cinnamon
- 1 ¼ cup granulated white sugar
- 1 tbsp heavy cream
- 2 tbsp unsalted butter softened

1. Preheat the air fryer to 350°F
2. Place the sweet potatoes into a medium sized mixing bowl. Add the salt, butter, egg, vanilla extract, ground cinnamon, white sugar, and heavy cream. Mix thoroughly for one minute
3. Place the pecans in a food processor. Chop the pecans until they are small and easy to sprinkle
4. Take the sweet potato mixture and place in a prepared 7" springform pan. Cover the top with the chopped pecans
5. Place the springform pan into the air fryer basket. Air fry at 350°F for 10-12 minutes or until the topping is browned

A I R   F R Y E R
Potato Wedges

PREP TIME: 10 minutes
COOK TIME: 20 minutes

INGREDIENTS:
- 4 Russet Potatoes
- 2 tbsp olive oil
- 1 tsp paprika
- 1 tsp salt
- 1 tsp garlic powder
- ½ tsp black pepper

1. Rinse and cut potatoes into wedges, leaving the potato skin on. Soak wedges in cold water for 25-30 minutes
2. After soaking, drain and pat dry
3. Coat potatoes with a tablespoon olive oil, paprika, salt, garlic powder, and pepper
4. Spread seasoned potato wedges into the air fryer basket, without overlapping
5. Return the basket to the air fryer and air fry at 400°F for 20-25 minutes
6. During the cooking process, shake the basket halfway
7. If you have larger wedges, 1-2 minutes of additional cooking may be added

AIR FRYER
Roasted Potatoes

PREP TIME: 5 minutes
COOK TIME: 20 minutes

INGREDIENTS:
- 24 oz petite potatoes
- 1 tbsp olive oil
- ½ tsp onion powder
- ½ tsp garlic powder
- ¼ tsp smoked paprika
- ¼ tsp white pepper
- ½ tsp ground black pepper

1. Rinse potatoes
2. Use a knife and cut the petite potatoes in half down the center. Toss with olive oil and seasonings to coat potatoes
3. Add potatoes to the air fryer basket
4. Air Fryer the potatoes at 400°F for 20 minutes, shaking basket halfway

AIR FRYER
Corn on the Cob

PREP TIME: 5 minutes
COOK TIME: 12 minutes

INGREDIENTS:
- 4 Corn on the Cob
- 2 tbsp unsalted butter melted
- 1 tsp salt
- 1 tsp pepper

1. Rinse corn and pat dry
2. Brush each ear of corn with melted butter. Then season with salt and pepper, to your taste
3. Place corn in the air fryer basket or on shelf
4. Air fry at 400°F for 12 minutes, turning corn halfway through cooking

AIR FRYER
Asparagus

PREP TIME: 5 minutes
COOK TIME: 8 minutes

INGREDIENTS:
- 1 pound asparagus
- 1 tbsp olive oil
- ⅛ tsp salt
- ⅛ tsp pepper

1. Rinse asparagus and trim the stems of the asparagus, cutting about 1-2 inches off the bottoms of each stem
2. Place the asparagus in the air fryer basket
3. Brush with olive oil, covering the asparagus with a light coat
4. Sprinkle salt and pepper, or desired seasonings on the asparagus
5. Place the basket in the air fryer and cook at 400°F for 8-10 minutes, depending on desired crispness

AIR FRYER
Cheddar Biscuits

PREP TIME: 10 minutes
COOK TIME: 5 minutes

INGREDIENTS:
- 2 cups all purpose flour
- 4 tsp baking powder
- ½ tsp salt
- ½ tsp cream of tartar
- 2 tsp sugar
- ½ tsp garlic powder
- ½ cup unsalted butter
- 1 cup shredded cheddar cheese
- ⅔ cup milk

Garlic Topping
- 2 tbsp unsalted butter
- 1 large garlic clove, pressed
- ¼ tsp garlic powder
- 1 tsp dried parsley flakes

1. In a large bowl, stir together the flour, baking powder, salt, cream of tartar, sugar and garlic powder
2. Add in the softened butter and stir with a fork until it is flaky
3. Stir in the shredded cheese and the milk, until it forms into a dough
4. Scoop or spoon a small amount of the dough into the basket, lined with parchment paper with holes in it, or a lightly sprayed with olive oil
5. Air fry at 400°F for 5-8 minutes, until biscuits are golden. To prepare the garlic topping, melt together the butter with garlic, garlic powder and parsley. Brush on the tops of the cooked biscuits. Serve warm

A I R   F R Y E R
Brussels Sprouts

PREP TIME: 5minutes
COOK TIME: 12 minutes

INGREDIENTS:
- 1 pound brussels sprouts
- 1 tbsp olive oil
- 2 cloves garlic pressed or minced
- ¼ cup shredded parmesan cheese
- ¼ tsp salt
- 1 pinch pepper

1. Preheat the air fryer to 400°F
2. While the air fryer is preheating, cut the brussels sprouts in half and rinse well
3. Place in a large mixing bowl, toss with olive oil and minced garlic
4. Place the prepared brussels sprouts in the basket, and sprinkle salt and pepper
5. Cook on 400°F for about 10-12 minutes
6. Sprinkle the parmesan cheese over the cooked brussels sprouts and return to the air fryer for one to two minutes, until melted

A I R   F R Y E R
Glazed Carrots

PREP TIME: 5 minutes
COOK TIME: 10 minutes

INGREDIENTS:
- 1 tbsp olive oil
- 8 ounces baby carrots
- 1 tbsp honey
- 1 tbsp brown sugar
- ¼ tsp salt
- ¼ tsp pepper

1. Lightly brush olive oil on the air fryer basket
2. In a medium bowl, stir together the honey, brown sugar, salt and pepper
3. Add the carrots to the bowl, and coat with the honey mixture
4. Place the carrots in the air fryer basket and cook at 400°F for 8-10 minutes

AIR FRYER
French Fries

PREP TIME: 10 minutes
COOK TIME: 14 minutes

INGREDIENTS:
- 4 medium Russet Potatoes
- 1 tbsp olive oil
- 1 tsp salt
- ½ tsp pepper

1. Peel and wash each potato. Slice them into strips, about ½ inch in thickness
2. In a medium bowl, soak the cut potatoes in cold water for at least 30-60 minutes
3. After they have soaked, drain the water from the bowl. Toss with olive oil and salt
4. Place half of the fries in the air fryer basket, without having them touch or overlap
5. Air fry at 380°F for 14-16, tossing halfway through cooking
6. Add an additional minute or two, depending on your preferred crispness

A I R F R Y E R
Onion Rings

PREP TIME: 10 minutes
COOK TIME: 8 minutes

INGREDIENTS:
- 1 large yellow onion
- 1 ¼ cup all purpose flour divided
- 1 tsp baking powder
- 1 tsp salt
- 1 large egg
- 1 cup milk
- 1 cup bread crumbs

1. Slice onion into ¼ inch strips. Remove center of the onion and divide the slices
2. Place onion slices into a large bowl or Ziploc bag. Add ¼ cup of flour and toss or shake the slices, coating each piece
3. Whisk egg, milk, baking powder and the remaining one cup of flour. Add the salt and bread crumbs into a second bowl. Dip each coated piece into the egg mixture, then dip into the bread crumbs, until coated
4. Place each coated piece into lightly sprayed air fryer basket, without overlapping or stacking the rings
5. Air fry at 380°F for 6-8 minutes, until coating is crispy

A I R   F R Y E R
Baked Potatoes

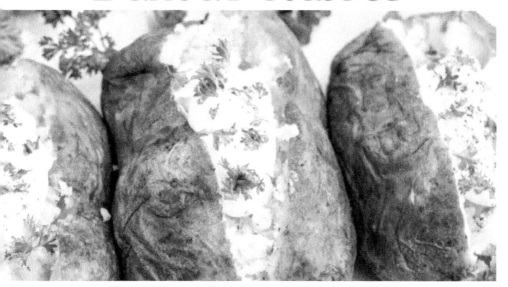

PREP TIME: 3 minutes
COOK TIME: 45 minutes
INGREDIENTS:
- 4 medium Russet Potatoes
- 1 tbsp Olive oil
- 1 tsp Kosher salt

1. Preheat the Air Fryer to 400°F
2. Lightly prick the skin of the potatoes with a fork and then rub the potatoes with olive oil
3. Cover the potatoes completely with the oil and then sprinkle kosher a light layer of kosher salt onto the potatoes
4. Place potatoes into the Air Fryer basket, leaving room in between each potato
5. Air Fry at 400°F for 40-45 minutes, rotating potatoes halfway through cook time
6. Carefully remove the air fryer potatoes and serve with your favorite toppings

Desserts

A I R   F R Y E R
S'mores Dip

PREP TIME: 3 minutes
COOK TIME: 6 minutes

INGREDIENTS:
- 1 cup chocolate chips
- 1 cup marshmallows
- 8 graham crackers

1. Fill the bottom of a 7" Springform pan or Air Fryer safe dish with ½ cup of chocolate chips
2. Top the layer of chocolate chips with the marshmallows
3. Cover the marshmallows with the remainder ½ cup of chocolate chips
4. Place the pan into the Air Fryer basket and cook on 350°F for 5-6 minutes. The chocolate should be soft and melting and the marshmallows should be a golden brow
5. Carefully remove the dish from the Air Fryer and serve with graham crackers or your other favorite dipping items

65

©AirFryingFoodie

Cookie and Cream Cheesecake

PREP TIME: 10 minutes
COOK TIME: 18 minutes

INGREDIENTS:
- 1 Package sandwich cookies, about 30 for crust, and 10 broken into large pieces, for the filling and topping.
- ½ cup unsalted butter melted One stick
- 24 ounces cream cheese softened
- 14 ounces sweetened condensed milk
- 2 large eggs
- 1 tsp vanilla

1. Line bottom of 7 or 8 inch springform pan with parchment paper circle, lightly butter the pan walls
2. Crush cookies in food processor, until they are fine crumbs. Combine with melted butter to form crust
3. Pour crust into pan, pressing the crust firmly to the bottom of the pan.
4. Beat cream cheese until smooth, slowly add in eggs, sweetened condensed milk, and vanilla. Mix until creamy
5. Pour over crust and spread evenly, pushing broken cookie bits into the filling. Top with cookie crumbs
6. Air fry at 300°F for 15 minutes. If center has a slight jiggle, return to air fryer and add an additional 2-3 minutes
7. Chill the cheesecake to chill for about 6-8 hours, or overnight

A I R   F R Y E R
Fried Sandwich Cookies

PREP TIME: 5 minutes
COOK TIME: 10 minutes

INGREDIENTS:
- 8 sandwich cookies
- 1 can crescents roll dough (8 count)
- 3 tbsp powdered sugar optional

1. Preheat the Air Fryer to 325°F
2. Remove crescent rolls from can and lay them out on a flat surface
3. Carefully wrap one cookie into each crescent roll sheet
4. Lightly spray pan with cooking spray, then add wrapped cookies onto the air fryer basket in a single layer, without stacking or overlapping
5. Air Fry at 325°F for 5-6 minutes, or the tops have turned until golden brown
6. Allow the fried cookies to cool for a minute before removing them from the basket
7. Sprinkle with powdered sugar and serve

A I R   F R Y E R
Cherry Pie Bombs

PREP TIME: 5 minutes
COOK TIME: 10 minutes

INGREDIENTS:
- 21 oz cherry pie filling
- 16.3 oz Grands biscuits
- 1 tsp cinnamon
- 3 tbsp granulated white sugar

1. Peel each biscuit into two layers, rolling each layer into a 4-inch circle, ending with 16 circles
2. Spoon a tablespoon of the cherry pie filling into the center of each circle
3. Pull the sides together and pinch to seal, then roll into balls
4. Lightly spray air fryer basket with a non-stick cooking spray, and place the balls into the basket about 2 inches apart
5. Spray the top of the balls with your cooking spray, or lightly brush with melted butter
6. Air fry at 350°F for 8-9 minutes, until golden brown
7. Combine cinnamon and sugar, then roll bites to coat

A I R   F R Y E R
Peanut Butter Cookies

PREP TIME: 5 minutes
COOK TIME: 5 minutes

INGREDIENTS:
- 1 cup peanut butter creamy
- 1 cup granulated white sugar
- 1 egg

1. Combine peanut butter, egg, and sugar, beating until smooth and creamy
2. Add a piece of air fryer parchment paper to the bottom of the Air Fryer basket
3. Use a 1 inch cookie scoop and scoop the dough onto the parchment paper. Use a fork to add crisscross marks
4. Place the basket into the Air Fryer and air fry for 4-5 minutes at 400°F, until cookies are lightly golden brown
5. Remove the Air Fryer basket and allow the cookies to cool for a few minutes before removing them and placing them on a cooling rack

69

A I R   F R Y E R
Chocolate Chip Pound Cake

PREP TIME: 10 minutes
COOK TIME: 15 minutes

INGREDIENTS:
- ½ cup butter
- 4 ounces cream cheese
- ¾ cup sugar
- 2 large eggs
- 2 tsp vanilla
- 1 cup flour
- 1 tsp baking powder
- ¾ cup chocolate chips

1. In a large bowl, combine the butter, cream cheese and sugar, mixing on medium to high speed until the batter is smooth and creamy
2. Add in eggs and vanilla, continuing to mix until combined
3. Slowly add in the flour and baking powder until it forms into a thicker batter
4. Stir in chocolate chips, making sure they are evenly mixed into the batter
5. Pour the batter into a lightly sprayed Bundt pan
6. Cook on 350°F for 15-18 minutes

Chocolate Bundt Cake

PREP TIME: 5 minutes
COOK TIME: 15 minutes

INGREDIENTS:

- 1 cup all purpose flour
- 3 tbsp sugar
- ½ tsp cinnamon
- ⅓ cup milk
- ¼ cup unsalted butter, melted (half a stick)
- 1 large egg
- 1 tsp vanilla
- ½ cup fresh or frozen blueberries

1. Combine flour, baking powder, and cocoa powder, then set aside
2. Beat cream cheese, butter, and sugar until cream creamy, about 2 minutes
3. Add eggs and vanilla to sugar mixture, once combined, slowly add flour mixture. Beat until smooth and creamy
4. Pour the batter into lightly sprayed or buttered Bundt cake pan.
5. Place pan in air fryer and air fry at 350°F for 15-18 minutes. Add additional increments of 1 minute if needed
6. Allow cake to cool for a few minutes, then carefully flip pan to remove cake onto a serving dish.
7. Cover with a chocolate glaze or frosting

A I R   F R Y E R
Chocolate Cheesecake

PREP TIME: 10 minutes
COOK TIME: 18 minutes

INGREDIENTS:
Cheesecake Crust
- 30 cookies crushed
- ½ cup unsalted butter

Cheesecake Filling
- 2 cups semi-sweet chocolate chips
- 3 8 oz cream cheese
- ½ cup powdered sugar
- 2 teaspoon cornstarch
- 2 large eggs
- 1 teaspoon vanilla

1. Line bottom of springform pan with circle of parchment paper, and lightly butter the pan walls
2. Crush cookies in food processor, until they are fine crumbs, then combine with melted butter to form crust.
3. Pour crust into the prepared springform pan, pressing firmly to the bottom of the pan
4. In a microwave safe bowl, melt the chocolate chips
5. Beat cream cheese until smooth, add powdered sugar, corn starch, eggs, and vanilla. Quickly stir in the melted chocolate
6. Pour filling over crust and spread evenly
7. Air fry at 300°F for 18 minutes
8. Allow cheesecake to chill to set, for about 6-8 hours, or chill in the freezer for about an hour

AIR FRYER
Apple Pie Bombs

PREP TIME: 5 minutes
COOK TIME: 8 minutes

INGREDIENTS:
- 15 oz Apple Pie Filling
- 12 oz Biscuit dough
- 4 tbsp granulated white sugar
- 1 tsp cinnamon

1. Split the biscuits in half and separate dough
2. Scoop a tablespoon of apple pie filling into the center of each circle. Fold in the sides, and then cover with the other half of the dough, and then roll into a ball
3. Combine the cinnamon and sugar mixture into a small bowl. Dip each dough ball into the cinnamon sugar mixture
4. Lightly spray air fryer basket and add the dough balls, seam side down in a single layer. Make sure to leave 2 inches in between each one
5. Air fry at 350°F for 8-10 minutes, until golden brown, turning halfway through cooking time

AIR FRYER

Brownies

PREP TIME: 5 minutes
COOK TIME: 10 minutes

INGREDIENTS:
- 2/3 cup all purpose flour
- 6 tbsp unsweetened cocoa powder
- 1/4 tsp baking powder
- pinch salt
- 3/4 cup sugar
- 6 tbsp unsalted butter melted
- 2 tbsp water
- 1 large egg
- 1 tsp vanilla

1. In a large bowl, stir together the flour, cocoa powder, baking powder, and salt
2. Add in the sugar, melted butter, and water. Stir together to combine the ingredients
3. Add in the egg and vanilla, stirring until the batter thickens
4. Pour the batter into a 6x6 pan, lined with parchment paper
5. Preheat the air fryer to 370 degrees Fahrenheit. Once it's preheated, place the pan in the basket
6. Cook at 370°F for 8-10 minutes

AIR FRYER
Red Velvet Cookies

PREP TIME: 5 minutes
COOK TIME: 5 minutes

INGREDIENTS:
- 1 Red Velvet Cake Mix
- 2 large eggs
- 1/2 cup vegetable oil
- 3/4 cup white chocolate chips

1. In a large mixing bowl, combine the cake mix, oil, and eggs. Mix until all of the ingredients are combined and it is a thick dough
2. Add the white chocolate chips and mix into the cookie dough until they are evenly distributed
3. Use a small scoop or spoon and drop scoops of dough into parchment paper lined basket of your air fryer Allow room for the dough to spread
4. Air fry at 370°F for 4-5 minutes per batch

Strawberry Cream Cheese Pie

PREP TIME: 5 minutes
COOK TIME: 6 minutes

INGREDIENTS:

- 1 refrigerated pie crust
- 1 cup strawberries chopped
- 2 tbsp white sugar
- 1 tbsp cornstarch
- 8 ounces cream cheese
- ½ cup powdered sugar
- 1 tsp vanilla flavoring
- 1 egg white

1. Preheat Air Fryer to 380°F
2. Beat cream cheese until smooth, add powdered sugar and vanilla
3. In separate bowl, toss chopped strawberries with sugar and cornstarch. Combine mixtures to make filling
4. Roll premade pie crusts. Using large cookie cutter or hand pie mold, cut dough into 4 circles
5. Scoop 2 tablespoons of filling into the center of each circle. Fold over until edges meet
6. Whisk egg white, then brush on inside edges of crust. Use fork or pie mold to crimp edges shut. Brush pies with remaining egg mixture
7. Air fry at 380°F for 6 minutes, flipping after 3 minutes

Ready for More?

Follow us as we share new recipes weekly
on our blog, airfryingfoodie.com

and

We would love to see YOU share in our
Facebook group,
facebook.com/groups/easyairfryerrecipesgroup

Happy Air Frying!

Printed in Great Britain
by Amazon

76254216R00047